Wisdom Of My Soul

A book with meaning, secrets and promises

Joseph Monk

BookLeaf Publishing

India | USA | UK

Made with ❤ on the BookLeaf Publishing Platform
www.bookleafpub.in
www.bookleafpub.com

Dedication

I dedicate this book to those who have unknowingly inspired these poems and unsaid words. To those who have far more importance to me than they would ever know

Preface

Poetry has always been a profound way to capture the essence of my deepest emotions and fleeting moments. In this collection, I have poured my heart and soul into verses that reflect the myriad experiences of love, loss, hope, and longing. Each poem is a piece of my inner dialogue my inner self, a fragment of my soul laid bare on these pages.

As you read through these lines, I hope you find a connection to your own experiences, and perhaps even discover new perspectives. May you find everything you are looking for in these poems.

Thank you for embarking on this journey with me. May these words resonate with you and bring a touch of poetry to your everyday life.

Acknowledgements

Thank you to everyone who showed genuine interest in my poetry, and for those who always encouraged me to keep on writing.
And thank you Mom and Dad for always being there.

1. Deep in the forest

Deep in the forest I stroll,
To hear the wisdom of my soul,
To think and weep and think some more, to pick the
path that I must take,
faced with a dilemma I cannot bear,
I pick the path that seems most fair.

2. Who's in the mirror?

In the mirror, a face I scarcely know,
Familiar eyes, yet shadows grow, Whispers of a self once
clear, Now fading into realms of fear.
Steps I take on paths unknown, Echoes of a voice, my
own, Lost in corridors of time, Searching for a rhythm, a
rhyme.
Memories like fleeting dreams,
Scattered threads in fractured seams, Who am I, this
ghostly guise?
A stranger in my own disguise.
Drifting through the days and nights,
Grasping at the fading lights, Pieces of a fractured past,
Slipping through my hands too fast.
Silent screams and muffled cries, Hidden truths behind
closed eyes, Yearning for a sense of place, In the void, I
search for grace.

3. Hollow man in hollow armor

A knight in hollow armor stands, A silent sentinel in
empty lands, His visage stern, his stance so grand, Yet
fragile is the heart he mans.
His steel, though forged in fiery breath, Cannot protect
from inner death, The weight of solitude he bears,
Behind the mask, a broken man.
For strength is but a fabled guise, When hollow echoes
are the prize, And in his silent, lonely fight, The hollow
man seeks but the light.
Perception's fooled by outer might, But in his core, there's
there's fading light,
For armor hollow, as is he,
Craves the warmth of company.

4. A blank sheet of paper

I'm looking at a blank slate of paper, wondering.. what will be drawn on it? Will it be majestic or simple, beautiful or not so beautiful, so white and unique I'd like to draw but no ink is in reach, this blank paper is much like my own life, time is passing by and I haven't made a mark on this blank sheet of paper, Not pure and not clean but blank, empty and bland wants to hold life on its page but not knowing where to start, I start with one line, oops that was wrong, back pedal, erase, now blank and empty agin. This blank piece of paper. With so many different options, that might all be the same, when they are all put together, it might have been better,Then a blank sheet of paper.But if I tried a little harder, to think of what to draw, then just maybe the page, won't forever stay white.And nether would my life.But just one little mistake, just one little tear, ssrrcchh goes the paper, one less picture, back to bare, I'm looking at a blank slate of paper.

5. Bright knight in the night

In the heart of the night, under the moon's pale light,
Rides a knight, clad in armor so bright.
With sword in hand, across the land,
He fights alone, in the sand.
Against the odds, he battles the gods,
In the silence, he nods.
His courage doesn't wane, despite the pain,
In his heart, hope does remain.
He fights for honor, he fights for right,
In the darkness, he is the light.
A medieval knight, in the lonely night,
His spirit shining, ever so bright.

6. All consuming void

In the depths of my despair, I dwell,
Disappointment engulfs me, like an unbroken spell.
I'm haunted by my failures, consumed by regret, No
glimmer of hope, just a void I can't forget.
Each step I take, burdened by my mistakes,
No solace or redemption, just a heart that breaks.
In this somber state, I find no peace, Only darkness and
sorrow, with no release.
The weight of disappointment, a heavy shroud,
No silver lining, no hope allowed
I'm lost in this abyss, drowning in my own pain, No
respite, no solace, just endless disdain.

7. The girl with beautiful eyes

In a world of colors, her eyes shine bright, Like stars in
the sky, they light up the night.
With a gaze so captivating and deep, Her eyes hold
secrets she's yet to speak.
They sparkle like diamonds, so pure and clear,
Drawing you in, making worries disappear.
With every blink, a story unfolds, A tale of love, of
dreams untold.
Her eyes, like windows to her soul, Reveal emotions that
words can't control.
They speak of joy, of laughter and grace, A reflection of
beauty that time can't erase.
So let us celebrate these eyes so rare, A gift from the
heavens, beyond compare.
For in those eyes, a universe lies,
A girl with beautiful eyes, a sight to mesmerize.

8. The man only God could kill

In a realm where mortals tread,
There lived a man, both brave and dread.
His strength unmatched, his spirit bold,
Legends of his might were told.
Through battles fierce, he stood his ground, With every
foe, he would astound.
But whispers spread of a prophecy, A man so strong,
only God could see.
His armor gleamed, his sword shined bright, As he faced
his final, fateful fight. with all of man under his feet,
there was only one left to defeat. as he clashed with
heavenly force, God's power proved to be his source.
With thunderous might, God struck him down,
A hero's end in a golden crown.
For even the mightiest can't defy, The will of God, the
reason why.
To be the last upon the throne his story told as the man
only God could kill.

9. Autumn is angry this year

Autumn what is that? I think I know.
Its owner is quite angry though.
He was cross like a cold bitter night
I watch him pace. I cry hello.
He gives his autumn leaves a shake,
And screams I've made a bad mistake.
The only other sound's that break,
Of distant snapping twigs and birds awake.
Autumn is normally joyful, compassionate and deep,
But he has promises to keep,
Tormented with nightmares of beaches and reindeer he
starts to prepare.
time is a promise a season should keep.
He rises from his longtime slumber, he slept too long!
With thoughts of pumpkins and Ghosts in his head,
A flash of rage and he sees red.
oh what little time he has to stretch his legs before a cold
winter sets in.

10. Cloak of sadness

Sadness, a weight upon my chest,
A heavy cloak that will not rest.
It weighs me down, it clouds my mind,
Leaves me feeling lost and blind.

It creeps upon me, uninvited,
A feeling that cannot be righted.
I try to shake it, let it go,
But it lingers, ebbing slow.

Oh sadness, why must you persist?
Why must you weigh me down like this?
I long to feel the sun once more,
To shed this cloak and close the door.

But for now, I must endure,
The weight of sadness, so unsure.
I'll wait for brighter days ahead,
And pray this cloak will soon be shed.

11. Natures artistry

As the day gently slips away,
The sky becomes a canvas, a grand display,
Streaks of orange, pink, and gold,
A masterpiece to behold.
The sun descends with grace and might,
Casting its warm and radiant light,
Painting the clouds with vibrant hues,
Creating a symphony of breathtaking views.
The world is bathed in a golden glow,
As the sun sinks lower, ever so slow,
A tranquil moment, serene and still,
A captivating scene, an artist's thrill.
Birds soar across the painted sky,
Bidding the day a fond goodbye,
The world holds its breath, in awe it stands,
As the sun slips away, to distant lands.
And as the stars begin to appear,
The sunset's beauty lingers near,
A reminder of nature's artistry,
A gift to cherish, for eternity.

12. Joy emerges

In the depths of sorrow, where darkness resides,
A flicker of hope, a spark that guides.
Through tears that fall like rain from above,
Sadness transforms, blossoming into love.

Grief may linger, heavy in the heart,
But joy emerges, a brand new start.
Like a phoenix rising from ashes below,
Sadness turns to joy, a radiant glow.

With each passing moment, a healing embrace,
Happiness blooms, painting a vibrant space.
Embrace the journey, the highs and the lows,
For sadness turning into joy, it truly shows.

13. A pickle named Pete

In a land of tasty treats, where flavors dance and meet,
There was a pickle named Pete, with a pickle-y beat.
He salsa-d with a taco, and tangoed with a pie, But his
favorite partner was a french fry, oh my!
They salsa-dipped and twirled, in a ketchup sea they
swirled,
A delicious dance that made the taste buds twerk and
twirl.
From the pizza parlor to the burger joint, Food and fun,
they never disappoint!
So grab a plate and join the feast,
Let's savor every bite, from the west to the east.

14. Movie romance

In the dim-lit room, I sit alone,
Watching movies on my own.
Laughter and tears fill the air,
But no one's there, it's an empty chair
Scenes unfold, emotions
rise, But there's an emptiness in my eyes.
I long for someone by my side,
To share the magic, the joy, the ride.
Whispered words and shared delight,
A hand to hold throughout the night.
But for now, I'll cherish these moments alone, Dreaming
of a movie partner to call my own.

15. True forgiveness

I feel a kind of hardness, God, encompassing my soul,
and where my heart was tender once, it now feels rather
cold.
I feel the invisible cuts, and I feel the pain that throbs, I
can see the hidden wounds and gashes, I lose the joy that
anger robs.
God reveals my bitterness and places it has grown, and
then He whispers in my ear,
"Forgive and let it go."

16. Death of a hero

In a realm where courage blooms, A hero's fate, the
darkness looms.
With every battle fought and won, Their journey ends,
their task is done.
Through trials faced, their spirit soars,
A beacon of hope, forevermore.
But as the sun sets on their quest, Their final breath, a
hero's rest.
The world holding their breath, hoping they didn't just
witness ... A hero's death
it appears dakrness won
Their memory lives in hearts and minds,
A legacy that time unwinds.
Though they may be gone from sight, Their bravery
shines, a guiding light.
So let us honor the hero's name, In tales and songs, their
deeds proclaim.
For even in death, their spirit lives on, A hero's legacy,
forever strong.

17. Digital world

In the realm of tweets and posts, Where likes and follows
matter most,
A world of endless scrolling, Leaves us feeling oh so
lowing.
Status updates and filtered pics, Creating a facade, a
virtual fix, But beneath the surface, we find, A weariness
that weighs on the mind.
Notifications, pings, and dings,
Constantly demanding our attention it brings, But in the
midst of this digital haze, We yearn for genuine
connections, always.
So let's take a break, unplug for a while, Rediscover the
joy that makes us smile, For in the real world, we'll find,
The true connections that soothe our mind.

18. Monsters come out at night

In the darkness, shadows dance,
As nightfall casts its eerie trance.
Monsters awaken from their sleep,
Their secrets held, their promises deep.
With gnarled claws and glowing eyes, They prowl
beneath the moonlit skies.
Their haunting whispers fill the air,
A chilling reminder of their presence there.
Beneath your bed, they patiently wait, Ready to pounce,
to seal your fate.
But fear not, for in the morning light, These monsters
fade, banished from sight.

19. solace in the cold

In the rain, I stand alone,
Drenched by tears from skies unknown.
Each drop whispers secrets untold,
As I find solace in the cold.
The world around, a blurry haze, But in solitude, my
mind finds ways.
To dance with dreams, to heal the pain, I find strength in
standing in the rain.
I embrace the storm, its gentle touch,
As nature weeps, I feel so much.
For in the rain, I'm not alone, I find a refuge, a place to
call my own.
I let the droplets wash away, The worries of another day.
And in the rhythm of the falling rain, I find peace, amidst
the strain.
So let the storm pour, let it pour, For in its embrace, I'll
endure.
Standing alone, in the rain's embrace, Finding beauty in
every tear's trace.

20. Poem inspired by Muhammad Bzeek

In the quiet halls of heartbeats' ebb, A gentle man walks, where angels tread.
Muhammed, the guardian of twilight's call, Cradles the fragile, through life's enthrall.
His arms, a haven for souls so light,
Bearing the children through darkest night.
Each breath, a whisper of love's purest form, A lullaby's warmth in the tempest's storm.
Though stars may fade in the velvet sky, Their light endures, in the tears he's cried.
For each precious life that slips away, Leaves a glow in his heart, night or day.
A mosaic of memories, bittersweet, Of tiny hands and silent heartbeats.Bzeek, a beacon of selfless love, Honoring angels called above.In the tapestry of existence so vast, His kindness, a thread, forever to last.
A tribute to those who've left too soon, Their spirits dance to an eternal tune.

21. Fallen king

Upon a throne of gold he sat, a king of great renown,
With subjects at his beck and call, and jewels in his
crown.
His words were law, his gaze was fierce, his power knew
no end, The world beneath his mighty feet, his kingdom
to defend.
But time, the silent thief of kings, did whisper in his ear,
A shadow cast upon his reign, a creeping, silent fear.
The crown that once shone bright and clear now dulled
with every day, The subjects who once praised his name
began to drift away.
And so the mighty king did fall, his empire turned to
dust,
The throne that once was gilded gold now tarnished with
mistrust.
Alone he sits, a fallen man, where once he ruled with
pride,
A king who touched the sky above, now lost within the
tide.